SINGLE AND SEEKING BOAZ

Love Relationships Of Women In The Bible

© 2017 By Veronica Paschal Moton

To Single Sisters Everywhere

CONTENTS

INTRODUCTION

What is there to say about dating? There is a lot to be said about it from what I'm hearing. Everybody is talking about it. Women are seeking Boaz, and men are searching for Ruth. Nonetheless both genders seem to be frustrated with trying to find a mate. Dating should be fun, but it seems that a process that should end in marital bliss is often times another fly by night fling some say. We all know that dating has changed over the years. There was a time when you could go out to a restaurant with friends and actually meet someone, but now we live in the age of technology, and a date is just one click away. Online dating makes it very difficult to focus on just one person. There are thousands upon thousands of profiles at ones disposal, where in my day we would work with the guy if we liked him. Nowadays you are dust if you don't get it all right the first time! Women or men really don't invest time in getting

to know each other, and why should they with so many

prospects at hand. So ladies, if you really want to find Boaz

you might need to take a look at some of the relationships in

the Bible, and the women who were in them. Let's find your

dating personality. You might just discover why you are

SINGLE AND SEEKING BOAZ.

SARAH

Now Sarah who was the wife of Abraham was faithful in all areas of her relationship. She was willing to allow Abraham to lead her even when it felt uncomfortable. She was completely committed to him even to the point of calling him lord. I know ladies, calling your future husband lord would in no way work in our time, but during that time it was a sign of respect and submission. However even Sarah suffered with impatience and insecurity. God had promised Abraham that he would be the father of many children, even as many as the stars in the heavens. Then Sarah because of her age laughed in disbelief. She did not believe the promise. After many years passed Sarah had still not conceived, so she decided to take matters into her own hands asking Abraham to go into her handmaid Hagar, and Abraham obeyed. Now even this was the plan of God because Hagar became pregnant and bare Abraham a son named Ishmael. He too became a great nation, although he was not the son of promise. However, I'd like to stop right here single ladies, and ask.....could your insecurity of age and desire for marriage be hindering you from capturing your Boaz? You are seeing your friends tie the knot, but still you have not met that special someone. Now you feel that it is urgent to meet Mr. Right so you have pushed to a decision of settlement. I must tell you if this is you, the decision that you will make will set the path of your life so choose wisely. When we are impatient and insecure we do not always put our best foot forward. Many times we can become resentful, withdrawn, distrusting, and even jealous. I have heard women say that it is all about how a man makes you feel. I agree, especially in a marriage, but here you are not in a marriage. You are just dating, so you have the advantage. If you are out on a date with a man who has a roving eye, please know that he is showing you who he is right then and there. If he is showing you on the first date that he cannot focus on you and make you feel like you are the only woman in the room after he has asked you out, know that it is a sign that this man is not one of loyalty, and as soon as you turn your back he will be chasing another skirt. I am not saying that people cannot change. It is up to you to take the chance on love, but trust me.....this behavior does not change overnight and you will undoubtedly suffer much heartache because of it. Never allow your impatience or insecurities to undermine the person that you are, or the plans that God has for you. When the right man comes along. He will make you feel everything you need to secure your emotions. You are not in an exclusive relationship just because you are on a date, you do not have to allow him to sabotage your enjoyment. If he is revealing himself on your date, let him. My suggestion would be to pretend you are in a movie theater and watch closely. Nine times out of ten if you say nothing, the film will keep rolling and he will think you're down with his behavior letting it all hang out! This my dear is a blessing to you because you will never have gotten a complete picture of the heart inside the man, sparing you from date number two. Anytime we allow insecurities to sabotage our emotional health, we give away our power to be our total selves in our relationships, as well as our ability to observe the character of the person we are seeking to become committed too. If a man is showing you he is not a person of loyalty, changing your hair, shoes, the way you dress, or character will not keep him. It is he who has to do the changing, and if he loves you enough, he will. It is as simple as that. So single ladies if you are dating a man and he does not make you feel emotionally secure when you are with him, nor is he exclusively settled on you, please know that you are not what he's looking for, and he is not your BOAZ.

DELILAH

I know. It is shocking to see her name here. I am not

suggesting in any way that any of you carry out the deeds of

Delilah. I am only focusing on the personality of the women

not occupation. I must say, and you must admit that there are

women who claim to be single and seeking Boaz who carry

these personality traits. Now Delilah was not faithful to

Samson, she was flirtatious, soothing, and cunning. Samson

loved her, and eventually told her his secret, then she

betrayed him. Ladies I know, we as women love to talk. We

love to share with our sister's, friends, and co-workers.

However if a man opens up to you enough to share matters of

the heart, please keep them sacred. His secrets are only for

you. I know that we all need a confidant, but please choose

wisely. I have personally heard women sharing very personal

details about the man in their life with co-workers, and

girlfriends and then wonder why he has stopped sharing with her or as we put it talking about what is in his heart. Well could it be that your confidant is Delilah, and she has gone behind your back and told him the very personal details that he shared with he thought only you? We all have that one special friend that we can share everything with, but you had better make certain she is your BFF even when you're not in the room. Remember, Delilah is double sided. She is loyal to no one, and that includes her sister friends. There is another attribute to Delilah that you will need to be conscious of as well. She was flirtatious! Most men like it when a women gets along with his male friends. Most times if the relationship elevates to a potential proposal you will see his buddies quite often, but no man wants a woman who feels the need to become the center of attention around his buddies. Again, this goes back to insecurity and the need to seek admiration from a place of disconnection within one's self. It is not a good look ladies for you or your guy. The dating arena is a time when all eyes are on deck, it's Ok to be cordial, but be careful not to send the wrong signals to a potential prospect. Believe me, he is watching. Honestly, most men do not know where the boundaries lie when they are around women. It will be up to you to keep them, so if you are making your way around the room speak and be polite, but make sure he is the center of your attention. If you have made it to the point where he wants to bring you around his friends, you are doing pretty good. That could actually be a sign that you will be around for a while so let's just say you've made it to first base. The other portion of Delilah's personality I find to be the most dangerous is. she was deceitful. Yes. Ms. Delilah was something else, and Samson with all his strength was not ready for her. She had been scheming with his enemies against him, and pretending to love him at the same time. She showed Samson the woman that he desired all while planning his demise. If you are the mother of a son, Delilah is not the woman you want him to bring home. Most Moms can spot her a mile off, and more than likely she has warned him to watch out! Most men love the Delilah's of the world. It's true. They fall head over hills in love with her, possibly because of her triple sided personality, and her ability to comply with whatever. Who knows? All I can say is they never see her coming, and before they knows it, she has hit them with a ton of bricks, leaving a mass of devastation behind. The only thing I will say is if Boaz ever sees this personality right up front, he won't be stopping at your door, and if he stops, he won't be staying, He's not looking for you.

3

VASHTI

Vashti whose name is interpreted (Beautiful Woman) was a Queen 485-465 B.C.E.). She was the daughter of King Belshazzar who became orphaned after his death, and given to King Ahasuerus to marry. There is a great amount of history in this story, so I'll just stay with our subject. Vashti is noted as defiant, and rebellious for not obeying her Kings' order when he summoned her to a party to be viewed by the Prince's, Noblemen, and other dignitaries of his Kingdom. Scholars give several reasons for her denial of the Kings' request. However, she was stripped of her position as Queen, and spent the rest of her days alone. If you would like to read more about her you can find the story in the book of Esther. However, let's talk about personality traits here. We know that she was intelligent, beautiful, argumentative, strong willed, and idealistic. Yes. There is a lot going on in the head of Queen Vashti, perhaps much more than is required for her own good. Ladies, these are marriages here, and I am not addressing my subject from a point of people who are married, only from the perspective of those who are single and possibly seeking marriage. If you are going to get your Boaz, you might have to be very creative in the way that you respond to him. Lol! I know ladies, but it is true. Even back then men did not think of or accept the idea of women as intelligent, and independent with a plan. Today nothing has changed. I find the biblical message of submission as serious though. When I was reading this story I could not help but read it through spiritual eyes. A King was to be obeyed, regardless of how one might feel, and disobedience was an immediate sentence of death. Therefore Vashti, because she was Queen was spared to even have lived out the rest of her days in the kingdom locked away. Anyway, as I stated there are so many interesting points to be made in this story, I only say that because of the scholarly commentary. However ladies when you meet a nice potential prospect, please do not embarrass him in front of his friends, or in public. That's what Vashti did, and so went her position as Queen. I don't know of many men who can stand up to being embarrassed or dishonored. A man wants to be honored. I must interject that to receive the honor he expects he must give it. If a man is truly considering to move forward with you he will respect you, and in doing so that means your request. So we know now ladies that Boaz is seeking a woman who will honor him. Boaz will tell you that he wants a women who is independent with a plan, because he is infatuated by your beauty, and he wants to impress you, but the minute you reveal you are more than just beauty, well…. let's just say he might just change his mind. I'm sorry, but the truth will set you free. When you are dating Boaz, please make him feel intellectually equal. Truth be told most men will say they want an intelligent woman, and perhaps he does but not one that displays it, at least from my experience. Maya Angelou is one of my favorite poets, and here is what she said, "People will forget what you said, People will forget what you did, But People will never forget how you made them feel" It's true. I can still remember the awkward moments that I experienced at a very young age. So just exchange the WORD people for he, and here is what you get, "He will forget what you said, He will forget what you did, But He will never forget how you made him feel." If you are dating Boaz and he does not feel he stimulates your intelligence, it will be his only perception of how you view him, and no one wants to feel like they are not smart enough. I know. It's just a small way to stroke his ego. As I said earlier, Vashti had been born into royalty. She was knowledgeable of all the customs and ordinances of the palace, while King Ahasuerus inherited his kingdom from his father Darius who had revolted her father's Kingdom and won. Perhaps she thought herself to be better because although he was King, royalty was not in his blood. He was merely an ordinary man in a crown. Now here is the problem ladies, Boaz was a man of wealth so when you are looking at him in regards to finances you are checking his pockets when you should actually be checking the richness of his soul. What I mean is you should be checking his character, but because the story tells us he was a rich man, most women are seeking someone of material value. Listen to me, I am not encouraging you to date someone who is not goal oriented, or unequally yoked. I am simply saying that dating someone with character is much more important than dating someone with finances who treats you like the garbage can where you put your trash. There are plenty of ordinary hard working guys out here with great character who will treat you with love and care. I'd rather ride in a Pinto with a man who truly loves me, than in a Maserati with a narcissist. If you will read the story of Ruth, you will find that Boaz was also a man of great character because he was willing to redeem the house of his kinsman. (Family Member) So ladies if you think you have a Boaz, while you are checking his status if that's your thing, please check for character as well. I found while reading the commentary some scholars imply that King Ahasuerus summoned for Vashti three times. I don't know how true that may be, but it certainly would have explained the reason for his wrath and harsh treatment of her other than the folly of his inebriation. Although she defied the King by not honoring his request Scholars also say that her choice in remaining in her quarters was because of Persian customs. We all know that this was the hand of God intervening to serve a divine purpose, nonetheless ladies, sometimes as women you may have all the right reasons for responding with an argument and still be viewed as wrong. What am I saying? I am saying to choose your battles wisely. There are times you just have to submit for the sake of honor, but after reading commentary on this one....Boaz would get an argument if he would ever ask me to sacrifice my character or moral values for his pleasure, so lock me away! Another side of Queen Vashti's personality was she was idealistic. While the King was partying with his boys, she planned her own entertainment. She was not expecting to be called to the party. Therefore ladies, if the phone is not ringing, plan your own entertainment, and move on. Do not sit around waiting by the phone as if he is already your Knight in shining armor! Get a life! If the phone is not ringing. He is not interested. Don't be the side chick who suddenly becomes interesting when there is nothing else to do, or no other love interest in his life. I see this with young women often, for the life of me I don't know how they put up with the shenanigans from these young men today. Most of them are just as deceitful as the Delilah's I talk about in chapter two. Let me be clear about this, I do understand while a lot of young women are choosing to move forward on their own. They are buying homes, cars, and starting businesses on their own because they just can't spend their lifetime waiting on a man who seems to have no interest, except for what they can get from them. That being said, there is still hope ladies, maybe you just have to broaden your scope and date outside racial boundaries. This is particularly true for black women. Black men have always dated interracially. However black women just can't seem to move across those boundaries. I am certain the reluctance is tied to somewhat of our history, could be we just don't feel the love. However ladies, if you are willing to go there the sky is the limit! My point here is whatever you decide to do, if he's not calling....MOVE ON! He is not your Boaz!

ESTHER

4

If I were going to say something about Esther to you ladies, I would tell you she was beautiful, pure, courageous, and cooperative. All of these women are described as beautiful, but we know that beauty lies in the eyes of the beholder. So let's take a look at some of the other characteristics of Esther. The Bible does not give a lot of detail about her character, but we know that she was pure. Now ladies....in that day to be a virgin until the time of marriage was a must! You would be stoned to death if you were not, and most times if a woman had been taken by a man she would be shamed and live away in isolation for the rest of her days. In todays' culture being pure, abstinence is seen as shameful. We see here how we have gotten away from what God deemed to be sacred only in marriage. It would serve society well if we would go back to doing things the way God had intended, perhaps we would not have the heartaches we have in our relationships or society today. I know the suggestion of abstinence is unthinkable in this day and time, but even a famous man wrote a book asking woman to abstain at least ninety days, and many of you listened to him, how much the more if God says it. Anyway, a little food for thought, maybe someone will consider it. Amen. Now that we've gotten that out of the way. Let's talk about Esther's act of courage. Esther had been sent to the palace to replace queen Vashti. She was chosen because of her beauty, purity, and cooperative nature. After her days of separation in preparing her to meet the King, she found favor with him and he made her his wife. Esther had a cousin who had raised her after the death of her father, his name was Mordecai who was of Jewish heritage and of the tribe of Benjamin. Mordecai was a keeper of the gate to the palace, and was of no respect of person. Haman who was chief of the army hated Mordecai because he refused to bow down to him when he returned from the Kings business, so he devised a plan to have the Jews destroyed. After hearing the news Mordecai sent a message to Esther telling her that her people were in great danger of being destroyed at the hand of Haman if she did not intervene, and to let it be known that she would not be saved, but would also perish if she did not approach the King on their behalf. So Esther harkened unto the counsel of Mordecai. Ladies there will be times when your dating relationship will be tested. Perhaps, he will lose a job, or have a family crisis with Mom or Dad. How will you respond? Are you willing to counsel him through it? If you run for the exit as soon as there is a problem, Boaz might change his mind about you if he was thinking of upping the stakes to a marriage proposal. Esther was not selfish, "she said if we perish we perish." I can tell you from experience, no one wants to be in a relationship by themselves. What I mean is some people as long as everything is going well and centered around them life is good, but let them have to sacrifice for your needs, as soon as the shoe is on the other foot there is a huge problem. Proving the relationship to be unbalanced, and guess who gets burned out.....Right! So be sure to have his back and prove that you do in your response in his crisis. As we know dating is the prelude to meeting the relationship you could possibly be in for the rest of your life, so once you decide to be exclusive, put your best foot forward. Many times Boaz will begin the dating process by asking you where you would like to go for entertainment, but as the relationship grows he will take you to places he enjoys as well. Be cooperative and show him your versatile side. You may not be big on guns, but if he wants to take you to a gun range, go! You might just find that you will enjoy it. If you would consider all that is happening in our world today, it may not be such a bad idea. A trip to a gun range may not be what you had in mind for a date, but learning how to handle a gun, and gun safety is a bonus. That's if you don't already know. Guys also like the idea that they can teach us girls how to do something that we don't know. It's like putting a stamp on us that they can say belongs to them, in other words, I taught you that skill. So girls if you are going to engage Boaz you will have to participate in some activities of his interest. That could include sports, such as football, basketball, pool, fishing, camping, hockey soccer, baseball etc. I know some of you ladies don't want to go anywhere that you can't wear shoes with heals, but there will be times when you will have to dress down. Remember, versatility. You want to show him that you will fit in whatever the occasion. Someone is looking at this right about now and wondering if all these qualities are necessary, but If you're going to ride with Boaz you'll not only have to be cute and polite, you will also have to have qualities that will make you stand out from the crowd.

5

JEZEBEL

The reason I am discussing some of these women is because their characters are opposite of what Boaz is seeking and you may not even know that the attributes of this woman is co- existing in your personality. Now that I have your attention, let's talk about Jezebel. Jezebel. Well the Bible has a lot to say about her. She was a priestess of the god Baal, married to the King Ahab of Israel. She was controlling, manipulating, deceitful, and even murderous. That right! You read it correctly. If you think Delilah is a force to be had even she has nothing on this Character. Ladies I would hope none of you with the attributes of this ladies character are seeking Boaz.

However we know that they are out there. Boaz be careful. This lady right here is seeking to control you and everyone in your life. She will stop at nothing to get her way. She preys on the weak, and those who will only sing her praise. She is seducing and colored with fascinating credentials. Her only desire is to be served. She will dress herself with pleasantries, but do not be deceived, kindness is not her friend, unless she can use it to manipulate you. Yes. Jezebel is full of games and some of them are deadly. Do not play with her unless you are ready to get burned! Let's hope this is not you. When I was researching Jezebel I did not know half the traits of this woman's personality. Now I know why she was so despised. It was because of her evil ways, Idol worship, and manipulating practices. If you are a controlling woman who feels that everything has to go your way or no way at all, that's a Jezebel trait. I know ladies that there are some men who set you up for this trait because they absolutely will not lead in anything. They are wearing the pants, and you are making all of the decisions, and so forth. It is not a good feeling believe me I know. However, if you have been dating this type for more than six months and he's still allowing it, get rid of him. He is not Boaz! Boaz is a leader. If you stay in that relationship the weight of carrying family, household, and other miscellaneous responsibilities will be left in your lap. They will span from keeping a roof over your head to making sure the oil is changed in your car. Listen, I don't know about you, but if I am going to have a man there are chores that I just will not do. They belong on his list, unless he is ill, and then someone else will do them. Now with that being said... if you have Jezebel traits you have a lot of work to do to clean up your act, and starting at an altar is not such a bad idea. In fact it is a good place to be begin. I don't even think you should be seeking Boaz until you clean up your act. This is not to say that you cannot change. Anyone who is willing can change their actions. God is able to help us in our weakness, but it is up to us to desire his character. It will not happen overnight, but as I said earlier if you are willing to change, God can help you, heal you of every hurt and pain. Some of you may have entertained these practices from a child. You were raised in an environment like Jezebel where certain behaviors were condoned, and they seem natural to you. It is the only way you know to be, but it is not natural. If your only goal is to take and to always take, to use and to always use, everybody and anybody that has a connection to this man, you might have Jezebel traits. If you want to separate him from his family or turn him against his family you might have Jezebel traits. If you do not appreciate the man that he is or the man that he is trying to be, you might have Jezebel traits, If you are turning him away from his moral obligations, and values you might have Jezebel traits. Please know that this book is written to inspire, not hurt. As I stated I do not know the reasons that bought you to a place where you only have a concern for yourself. However I do know that if you are willing God can change you and make you whole. He can create within you a new heart. A heart that will feel love, give and receive it from others. He can help you to turn away from seeking and taking pleasure in your own ways and give you new direction if you'll allow him. He even gave Jezebel room to change, but she would not, but you can do it. You can turn your life around. If you will give your heart to Jesus right now. All you have to do is tell God you are sorry for all the pain you have caused, all the wrong you have done to others, and ask forgiveness, Amen.

6

LEAH

What is to be said of Leah except that she got caught up in the
scheme of her father Laban, She was innocent yet faithful to Jacob
all her days. As the story goes, Jacob had work for Rachel seven
whole years, and when he was to receive her as his wife Leah was
given to him instead. It was customary for the first born to married
first. Jacob without knowledge of the customs perceived that he
would marry Rachel, Laban's youngest daughter, and Leah's sister.
So here we have a family entangled in Laban's plot of deception.
Can you imagine how Leah must have felt knowing that she was not
his first choice, and that his love was not for her, but for her sister?
She had to be strong to endure such pain. Can you imagine the
anger towards her by Jacob even though it was not her fault that

she was traded and used as a substitute to pay for Jacob's labor by Laban? This is how it is when you are dating a man that you really like and he has eyes for your friend. It happens ladies, and you should not choose passivity in this situation. Many times it has nothing to do with you, but rather choice. I do understand that it could be a bit personal for you when this happens, it could be both very sticky and tricky. Personally I say he's out! However, there are people who have the special built in capabilities of being able to pass the buck. I really believe it has to do with ego, especially when the friend knows that you really like the guy, but will choose to date him anyway. I'm dating you, you like my friend, BYE! If your girl is not telling you to get rid of him, WATCH her, she has the face of Delilah, and the Traits of Jezebel! True friends want nothing but happiness for their Girls. If you are out with your girls and you are all looking at the same guy it's a matter of flavor. If he approaches you, eyes of ladies, he is not your Boaz. He has clearly made his choice, so any moves to procure his attention by friends after he has made his selection is an obvious sign of disloyalty, Boaz has chosen. I understand that there may be someone asking the question of what about in marriages when the husband makes a pass at the best friend? Remember, I am not addressing people in marital relationships, but for the sake of an answer I will say, please be very careful. I would check him vehemently so that he would know to never try it again. It is very obvious that something is going on in the relationship, and you are not to intervene, then I would remove myself allowing space for healing if it possible for it. If you decide to tell your BFF please know that there is a possibility that you will become villain and the friendship will end. Also please be aware that if he is making a pass at you he has undoubtedly made passes at other women and your friend already knows of his disloyalty to her, but has not mentioned it to you. We are women, and we know our man. I am sure if you check him and give him a pass for his scandalous behavior, you will have possibly saved a marriage, as well as your friendship. Always look pass your selfish desires. If your friend has a hubby who is being unfaithful, she will need your shoulder, as well as your confidant ear. While reading the story of Jacob, Leah, and Rachel you will find that Jacob meets Rachel first and falls in love with her upon first sight. The story takes a turn when Laban intervenes or breaks his promise to Jacob giving him Leah instead. FAMILY!! In most cases Laban's character would be the mother of Boaz, just look at how Rebekah preferred Jacob and schemed with him to receive the promise intended Esau. Yes ladies look out for Boaz's mom. Hopefully she will respect his choice, but if she does not let the drama begin!! LOL! I am sorry moms but we can bring the drama when we don't agree with our children's choices in relationships. However, if Boaz has made his decision, it will be his place to tell his family to back off, and that includes you mom. It is very difficult to maintain a dating relationship that is elevating towards marriage when there is family discard regarding ones choice, so the faster he can bring this issue to resolve the better it will be for you. However, if he is lingering about the situation and it is festering to the point where family is being disrespectful to you, you may want to let Boaz move on. There is nothing more hurtful than having a man who says he loves you, but will not defend your honor, knife cuts both ways folks, if he truly loves you he will rise to the occasion. You also have to observe interactions closely ladies, because maybe Boaz has told his family that you are just around until he meets the real deal. Maybe you are Leah and Boaz has a heart for someone else who he's keeping secret that family members are aware of. Yes! Maybe you are his in between fling! There are so many young women still in relationships with guys they know are not interested in them. If he does not want you, move on and find someone who will appreciate you. God knows you deserve to be loved. Love yourself enough to MOVE FORWARD! Please accept that he is not your BOAZ! This may have been a subject for a previous chapter, but BOAZ will not already have a wedding band on his left ring FINGER! He will not belong to another woman. He is not your Boaz if he is MARRIED. There are too many single women seeking Boaz in another woman's home. That's right I said it! Get your own man, and leave hers alone! He is just using you. I do understand that there are times when he has not revealed to you that he is married, but you are not that naïve. If he can only see you a certain time of day or night, he barley calls unless he is at work, he always speaks to you away from his home, you cannot visit his home, he cannot spend time with you on holidays, etc....HE"S MARRIED! Now you know so there is no excuse. Boaz is single. He's not living with anybody. He may be divorced, but he is SINGLE! AMEN. Now that you have the scoop on his choice, family and their interventions, I think we are allowed to move on to our next subject.

7

RACHEL

Rachel was also put in a predicament not of her own will. No doubt

Jacob had mentioned to her that he had asked her father for hand in

marriage. I can imagine that she was very happy of the news, and

expecting to become his wife. However after learning news of what

her father had done, I can understand how resentment would

become a part of her everyday life, in other words Rachel became

jealous, and envious of her sister. I say that to make the point of

sometimes things are completely out of his control. If you admire

your date and find him attractive, please know that there are other

women who will find him attractive as well. You are out on the town

and your mate has your hand walking into the venue when Miss.

bold pushes in front of you so that she can be seen. He glances at her and then back at you pulling you closer, what would you do? Listen, he is not dead, and you don't know what his thoughts are. As long as he remembers he is your date and his eyes does not bulged to the point that it becomes disrespectful to you, I say let him look. He turned his attention back to you, meaning that his eyes are for you, and you will end the night on that note. So don't get upset over every little episode you encounter while out learning each other. If you get angry every time your man looks at a women.....well you might just need to remain single. Your goal at this point is to learn his mannerisms while enjoying his company. I must say too that you do have the guys who have not made you feel secure in the arena of your emotions. They are the ones to watch. These guys are real characters with big egos. If you are going to be with one of them you had better know that they are lovers of all women, and are seeking to secure none. He will never be Boaz because he thinks he is the gift not you! He parades himself around women as if they are priviledged to be in his company. You'll know him right off. He is what we use to call a Player because he plays with your emotions, he never secures them. He will come in disguise with all the outward appearance of an angel to attract you, but his character is like his woman twin Jezebel! Run Ladies! The only real interest he has in you is your level of ability to serve him. He is not Boaz and he will only leave you Broken and Shipwrecked! However, there are times ladies when we bring our own drama to the arena. Boaz has proven to you that he only has eyes for you, and you are asking him for what he does not have or cannot control. Jacob had proven to Rachel that he loved her without failure. He worked seven long years for Laban to have her as his wife. However because she was barren and her sister was able to give Jacob children, Rachel would not allow peace in her home, but troubled Jacob night and day over giving her children. Sometimes ladies we will not allow ourselves to reach the point where Boaz will even feel comfortable enough with us to move further in the relationship, because we are so insecure about pass issues we have encounter with an Ex. I have heard on countless occasions young men say I would love to date her, but she has too much baggage. I know, Knife cuts both ways right. However the name of the book is SINGLE AND SEEKING BOAZ, we will pick up on his journey to seek Ruth next Book. All things aside ladies, if I am going to be real with you, you are going to have to let the past go, so you can get past the first date. No one wants to be on a date with you and all you do is talk about your Ex and how he did you wrong. I am not saying that he should be unsympathetic to your pain, but you are trying to establish rapport with him. If you have to talk about your ex anything the night is not going in the right direction. Your Ex is not there. Therefore he should not be used for a fill in for conversation. After all, you want him thinking of you and not his ex. So, Rachel had quite a few situations to deal with considering Jacob was totally committed to her. There will be times when this may happen, especially if you are dating a man who was previously married or one who has children by another woman. I can tell you from experience, blended families are not easy. If you are with a man who has children by another woman, you will have to be extremely careful when communicating with him about his children provided that he cares for them. If he is really an active participate in their lives, you will have to understand that every weekend will not belong to you. If he is truly a single parent as some women are then there are other responsibilities that he will have to engage. However, his actions can sometimes be very tricky so watch closely. I take you know what I mean, but I'll go ahead and spell it out, he is playing both sides. If he shows an inkling of straddle the fence behavior, this is a man who is playing with your emotions, and he is definitely not your BOAZ.

8

RUTH

Finally our last personality. There is a lot to be said about Ruth. I have chosen to describe these women with the characteristics I see when reading each of their stories. You may see other words that describe their personality as well. I see in Ruth courage, kindness, loyalty, and initiative. Let's talks about her courage. Ruth was a Moabite who married Mahlon the son of Naomi who had moved with her husband Elimelech from Bethlehem during a famine. Upon their arrival they found the city of Moab to be prosperous and found that there was enough work to provide food and shelter for their family. Nevertheless they were Israelites in a strange land. Soon after they arrived Elimelech fell sick and perished. Naomi remained in Moab ten years with her sons Mahlon, and Chilion his brother then they both perished, leaving Naomi alone to care for her two daughters, Ruth and Oprah. So Naomi decided to leave Moab and return home to Bethlehem because she had heard that the famine had ended, and Ruth her daughter in-law pleaded to return with her. Ladies sometimes you will have to have the courage enough to leave Moab. You will have to leave the dead relationships behind for a new beginning. Ruth showed extreme courage in letting go of the only life she had ever know to reach for what could be. She left behind her friends, her culture, and the only home she knew in hopes of having a better life. She said, "I will follow you wherever you go, Your God will be my God, and Your people my people". Wow! Are you ready to be that committed? It might just be that Boaz is in the military. He may have to leave the Country and ask that you come with him. What if he takes a job in another state, are you willing to go with him. You must think of these things if Boaz is really starting to look like a final option. Is this someone you love? Is this someone you can live with? Hopefully by this stage in the process you will have the answer. Ruth was also kind. She loved her mother-in-law and took it upon herself to take care of her. LOL! I laugh because this type of relationship is rarely seen between mother and daughter-in-laws. There is normally a power struggle between the two women, but anyway, Ruth loved Naomi so much that she was willing to sacrifice everything she knew to go with her. Listen ladies, most guys absolutely adore their mother's, of course you have your dysfunctional relationships, but for the most part this is not a relationship you want to challenge. I have heard women say, "I'm not second fiddle to his mom." No! You are not, but give mom her space. He should not have to choose between his mom and you and if he is forced to you are already starting off on the wrong foot. I hear women always telling their girlfriends, "Girl he's a Mama's boy", not to make excuses for him, but maybe his relationship with his mom is the best relationship he has ever had with a women. Maybe the women he has been involved with have been users, Delilah's or Jezebels. Maybe he needs to know that he can trust you, and he will need a little help with that. Boaz may just need to find the right woman, and your kindness will help him to see that woman is you. Ok. I know I said you need to help Boaz out by showing him your kindness, but what he really needs after Jezebel and Delilah is your loyalty. If you read the chapters on those two ladies then you know why. There is nothing like a woman who will have her man's back, float or sink, believe me you'll be tested during the dating process and Boaz will be watching. It is important to him to know before he escalates to an engagement that he can trust you to be by his side. I think it good to at least experience one challenging ordeal that you will have to work through before he gets an engagement ring just to see how you will handle it. However, that's my personal opinion. I can tell you if you would interview a hundred men asking them the top five qualities in a potential partner loyalty would be pretty high up on the list and we're only talking top five. If you can't be trusted there really is not a relationship. Trust is everything. Look, I know that you are probably asking yourself why you should put it all out there for someone you are just dating, but you are not just dating anybody baby, you are dating Boaz, and he is a heart of gold kind of guy. I'm not talking from a point about the fact that Boaz is financially sound, I am more so talking about his character. He is a really good man who will have nothing but good intentions for you. That being said, you do not have to fear letting him see the real you, in fact he wants too. Ruth also was a woman of initiative. She asked to go into the field to glean. If you and the fellow you are dating are more exclusive and his family is having an event ask if you can help. Even if the answer is No. Your Boaz will see that you don't mind pitching in if necessary and I am sure he will find you more attractive for asking. Guys love when the woman they bring around their family connects and feels at home. It makes it easier for him to relax and act as host. So whatever the cause don't be afraid to speak up. Now listen, if you know that you have just started to date this guy, please don't start taking over his personal space. Don't go to his house and do his laundry. Make sure he has settled on you before you begin to offer help in anyway. Remember you have Jezebels twin who will take extreme advantage of any kind offer that you make. Remember the character of Boaz. You may offer, but Boaz is a man, he will not let you do anything he feels is improper. In conclusion ladies I have given you eight women of the Bible that had telling signs that kept them from enjoying the full potential of their relationships. These are the same characteristics that will keep you from getting the man you'd like to have in your life while dating Mr. Right. It's not hard to know when you are in the right relationship because all these qualities will come with it. Sometimes you will have to work to get the kinks out, but if you are dating a good guy you will know because he will be doing most of what I discuss in these chapters. So observe, listen, move slowly, and be patient. Boaz is out there and he is looking for YOU.

www.ingramcontent.com/pod-product-compliance
Lightning Source LLC
Chambersburg PA
CBHW021121020426
42331CB00004B/572